Humorous
Essays

By Tracy Burch

To order additional copies of this book, contact:
Xlibris Corporation
1-888-795-4274
www.Xlibris.com
Orders@Xlibris.com

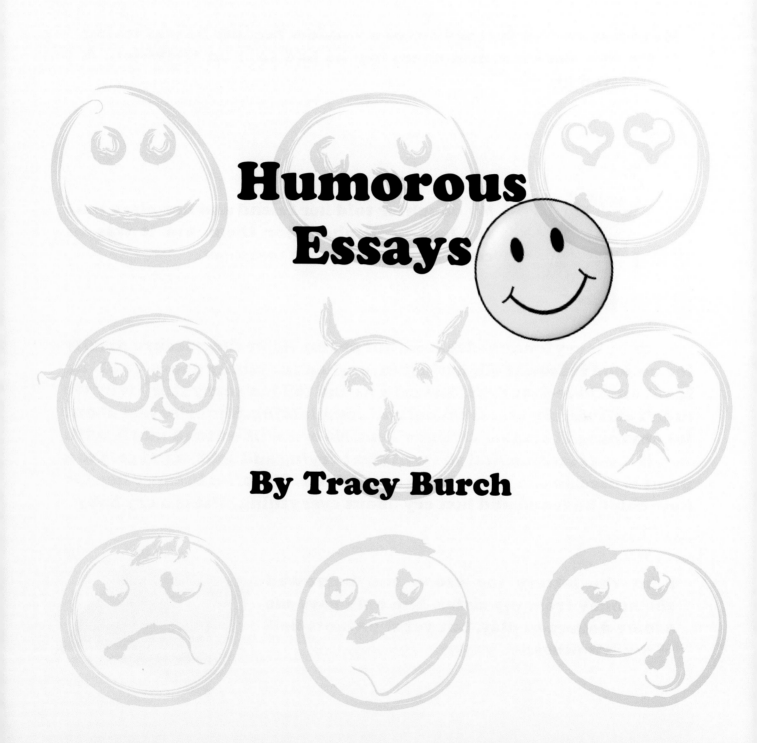

Humorous
Essays

By Tracy Burch

My oldest brother jumped out of a window because he was trying to fly like the superman character he had seen on television. A bush saved his life.

My daughter told her friend and her niece that she had a cell phone for them, but it was an empty box. They were so up -set.

Most people cry for a good reason, but not my sister she cries practically for no good reason at all, for instance when the family doesn't call her for about three-four days. She calls us and tell her sorry story why we didn't call and she starts crying and complaining. She cries just about for anything. It creates a big problem. No one will watch a movie with her. If it gets sentimental she will start crying and sobbing. It gets to a point where no one wants to be around her. She cries because her car keys can't be found and just cry about everything. She is a cry baby.

I hit the lottery for $1000 and borrowed the money from my sister. She only gave me $10.00 dollars to play, but yet she wants half of my winnings.

I have seen some people moving into an apartment. They had very filthy mattresses and I wondered if their whole apartment is filthy.

My fiancé Elvin was going to the store to play lottery. It was raining and I didn't want him to get wet so I let him borrow my umbrella. At first I hesitated because he is so forgetful   my conscious was telling me not but I gave it to him any way. He left it in the store came back he was only gone for a second my umbrella was gone. I think the workers stole it. Then, every time he wants to borrow something from me I say No!

My son James was invited over his friend Grabriel house for a sleep over. Then the next day his mom called me and said that my son ate their whole ham. I didn't believe her, but I did not want any chaos. She wanted $20 dollars for my son eating their ham and I gave it to her.

My daughter asked her step-father to wash her bra. She said I had it on for 3 days. He told her to wait until mom gets home. He couldn't stop laughing.

One day I was driving in the car. I had my fiancé, 6 year old daughter, granddaughter with me. Then my granddaughter passed gas. Instead of my daughter opening the window. She moved over and sat beside my granddaughter. Me & my fiancé started laughing we laugh so hard My fiancé farted too.

When I was in college my instructor was in the process of giving us a test the following week. I said to the instructor could we have an open book test as a joke, but I wasn't prepared and received a failing grade. I had studied for the original multiple choice test.

My fiancé went to play lottery the Mega million. The next day he couldn't find the ticket so we were looking in the trash and all over the house. Then finally, he found it on the side of the end table in our bed room. Each day he misplaces or loses everything from keys, socks, underwear, glasses you name it.

One day he was drinking liquor and drank it up so fast. He accused me of drinking it up, but I don't drink liquor. He has known me for five years.

One day my son was sitting at the table. My fiancé ask my son for a slice of pizza. He said No! this is all I have.

My sister is scared of elevators and I guess she watches too much television. Every time we go places there is an elevator. As result, she walks up flights of stairs. Then one day I finally convince her to get on the elevator in the process, she squosed me so tight. I thought that I couldn't breathe and this was so embarrassing.

One day my fiancé was making my daughter a peanut butter & jelly sandwich. He had use pumpernickel bread, and my daughter said to him I don't want any burnt bread you burnt up the whole loaf.

Every time I turn around I get hot flashes. Then my fiancé would say what's wrong I answer and he opens all the windows in the house, but it's in the winter. I have to explain to him that I have a little portable fan. This situation happens all the time.

I woke up in the morning brush my teeth, combed hair, then rushed to Meyers. When I got home I noticed toothpaste on my mouth and it dried up. I was wondering why the lady in the store grinned at me and started laughing.

Me and my son was walking thru the mall and my son pants fell down to his knees we were still walking I didn't notice until I got to my car.

Me and my son was on the city bus. He saw a man with a hole in his shirt and said loudly. Why does he have a hole in his shirt? The people on the bus started laughing.

Me and my son was in Kmart and he saw a woman with very long fingernails that curled up. He said loudly ugh! That is nasty.

Me and my daughter, two granddaughters just return home from an outing. As I was parking the car I thought my 3 year old granddaughter open the door. I almost panic, but she was just taking her seat belt off and it hit the door.

My instructor brought a picture of his new baby to class. The baby had a big spot on his face. I asked what's wrong with the baby? A classmate said it's a birth mark what is your problem!

When I was in college I took the same course by mistake. Then when I found out I was in the middle of the course. Of course I dropped the class.

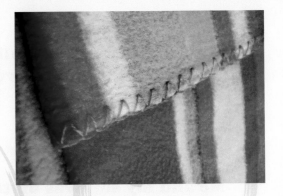

While I was shopping for clothes my baby was in her stroller crying. I couldn't calm her down and then a lady came over to me and gave my daughter a bright blanket and she stopped crying immediately.

I was in Rite Aide one day and made a transaction with my debit card. I told the cashier specifically, to just take $20 dollars off my debit card and I will pay the difference. I told her twice, but she still made an error of putting in the whole amount of my purchase on the card. I had to call my bank immediately. If people would just take their time things would get done right. There was no one behind me.

My friend lost her house keys one day. Then her daughter said to her that she must have left them at the casino. She was being sarcastic.

One day my step-father was arguing with the man down the street. My step-father said to him. Do you want your shirt dirty? Then the man ran in the house.

My mom always calls me to tell me her corny jokes. I had to make myself laugh.

One day my fiancé was looking for his glasses, I said to my fiance that the glasses is on his nose.

I was in the fitting room at the mall. Then I realized that a little boy was looking under the door at me. He surprised and scared me.

I was in the store one day and seen kids ripping open the toys. I went and got the manager some people will not say a word.

When I get sale calls I would tell them 12th prescient or say if I wanted to buy anything I will call you and then hang-up.

One day my friend borrowed $20 dollars from me two months went by and she never gave it back. So I saw her coming out of the bank as I called her name. She acted like she didn't hear me. Then I ran up to her and she gave me my money.

Me and my friends were going out to a club it started raining in the process. I ran over a deep pot hole and didn't notice that I have gotten a flat until the next day. I guess the air was seeping out slowly, but surely.

Every time I get on the phone my fiancé is right there listening so I go into the bathroom and talk and he gets angry. Then one day I flip the script.

One day while I was driving in the city of Detroit I was dodging pot holes then the police pulled me over and gave me a ticket. I had to explain to him that I was not under the influence of alcohol. I should have gotten the bumper sticker off of my old car it read "I am not drunk I am dodging pot holes"

Every time I tell my son to wash the dishes he leaves the dirty pots on the counter. Then have an excuse. When he asked me for money I would have an excuse too.

Me and my mom was going to buy my daughter a bike. We called a cab and hold a conversation all the way to our destination. When we got to our destination. She put $20 dollars in the slot. The cab driver said that my mom didn't give him any money she yelled and said that she is going to call the police and get his cab number. Then the situation changed and he suddenly, found the money.

My grand-daughter went to school one morning ate a good breakfast, but for lunch she had just a cold cheese sandwich not a grilled cheese and the other kids had chicken Mcnuggets and milk. I guess the school got my grand-daughter on a diet.

My brother hit the mega millions and didn't give his mother a dime. I invited him to my daughter's birthday party and he gave her just $5 dollars.

He told me he bought a house in Bloomfields Hills that is what he said, but it's not true. He gave me the wrong address. My mother told me he live somewhere else.

My friend is very motivated to clean her house, but not to get a job to better herself. She loves to have house parties with her family & friends all night till dawn to dust and loves to shop till she drops especially for clothes, but doesn't have enough money. I believe she is dreaming of a fairy tale life and needs to pursue an education. She feels that she is not smart enough, yet she can manipulate people out of their money, especially men actually, she is not my friend.

I called my landlord to tell her that I had a broken pipe in the basement. She came, but brought her two kids. They were so hungry and were going into my refrigerator. She is so unprofessional and the job didn't get done.

One day my sister went to an amusement park rode the rides. Then the next day she had a headache for two weeks.

She called me and told me about the incident and finally realized that she have high blood pressure and was taking pills three months before.

One day me, my fiance and my daughter was visiting my sister and her family for christmas. I brought my wine from home and they helped drank it up. They offered us food, but not anything to drink, As a result we almost choked. When I looked into her refrigerator it was full of beer, wine and liquor.

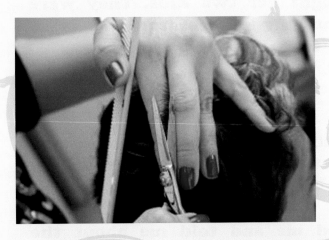

At one time I went to another hair salon and the beautician cut too much of my hair off. About two weeks later I went back to the same salon and requested another hair dresser to service me. While I was there I got on the conversation of short hair and told the other stylist that a lady at another salon jack me up and cut off too much hair I only wanted my ends clip. Then the lady who did my hair was right there next to me working on her client hair. She said to me that I am talking about her. I said that is not true and she kept repeating herself, but actually I was.

My daughter have a boy in her classroom who takes her hat out of her locker and throws it away. He also rips up her homework report card and throws it back in her locker. I told my daughter that he likes you, but need to show it in a different way. At first I wanted to tell my daughter to do the same to him, but I wasn't raised that way.

My daughter was in preschool they had an Easter egg hunt. She found all the eggs and the teacher asked her to share with the other kids. Her respond was why I found them.

One day I let my daughter borrow my car for a graduation dance. She brought the car back damage and told me someone hit her while parked. I believe she lied and can't drive.

On a particular day I let my son drive me to the store for the first time and he turned the corner very sharp I thought I was having a panic attack and told him to slow down.

My granddaughter told my fiance that when her mom whips her.
She pretend like it was hurting and go into the bathroom put water
on her face. She said I faked her out.

About the Author

Hi, my name is Tracy Burch and I came from a family of five three sisters and two brothers born in Detroit. My mother always taught us to be positive and do not let anyone get in our way of success. She taught us that life is full of challenges and obstacles and we have to be strong.

I have five children, also like my mom it's just a coincidence. I have three girls and two boys they are a blessing to me, and is my inspiration in day-to-day life. I just love them so much and they know it. I would like to thank my mother because without her I wouldn't be here on earth today to tell my story. I appreciate her loving and support throughout my career and her love for me is unconditional. I also would like to thank my children for giving me a reason to keep striving with hope and aspiration even though I can be very stressed at times.

To my siblings I love you all so much. I don't know what to do without you. I know life is an adventure but dealing with a sister like me who refused to grow-up is an adventure too.
I found that I have become more creative when writing short stories, poetry and to use my imagination to the best of my ability. Also, to write from experience. I learned how to appreciate poetry, non-fiction stories and fiction stories and hope it will inspire others writers to write about their experience.

When I was in college I registered for electives classes, which was English, The Creative Writer and Poetry. While, receiving my papers I always receive high grades. I entered one of my short stories into a contest and won second place. This is when I found my talent to become a writer. Although, it was later in life because of my age, but it's never too late.

One of my instructors encouraged me to become a teacher because I would always put an extra effort into my research papers by adding extra words to make it more intensive. Isn't it very interesting and wonderful how a person can encourage you to dig deeper into your talent? Sometimes a person doesn't even notice they have a talent unless someone brings it out into the opening. Maybe a parent, aunt, uncle or best friend can give you a little push to explore a passion or talent. While being in college I decided to pursue an extra career in communications   why did I go this route. Along the way I took a class in journalism in 2008. I felt confident that I had what it takes to be successful, but my instructor would always give me a D grade. He never told me to write as a 10th grader when writing papers. I was shocked and embarrassing and thought how can this be. When I first started class he should have told the class to write as if we were in the 10th grade As a result, my grades would have been a much better. I didn't put my name on my paper at one time and when he called all the students to get their papers. He didn't call mine. I address him and saw the E grade I was so very shocked. I dropped the class too soon. I should have asked more questions. I thought of myself as a failure. As time went by I got over it and became an excellent writer.

Printed in the United States
by Baker & Taylor Publisher Services